Ebb Tide—Flood Tide

Marshes at flood tide.

Ebb Tide–Flood Tide

Beaufort County . . . Jewel of the Low Country

Photography by Lynn McLaren

Preface and Epilogue by Lynn McLaren
Additional Text by Gerhard Spieler

HILLSBORO PRESS

Originally published by the University of South Carolina Press. Copyright
1991 by University of South Carolina

Printed in Hong Kong through Palace Press

99   98   97   96   95   5   4   3   2   1

Library of Congress Cataloging-in-Publication Data

McLaren, Lynn, 1922-
    Ebb tide—flood tide: Beaufort County . . . jewel of the low country
/ photography by Lynn McLaren ; preface and epilogue by Lynn
McLaren ; additional text by Gerhard Spieler.
       p. cm.
    1. Beaufort County (S.C.)—Description and travel—Views. 2. Sea
Islands—Description and travel—Views.   I. Spieler, Gerhard.
II. Title
F277. B3M35 1991
975.7'99—dc20   91-21741

ISBN 1-881576-47-7

Published by
HILLSBORO PRESS
an imprint of
PROVIDENCE HOUSE PUBLISHERS
238 Seaboard Lane • Franklin, Tennessee 37064
800-321-5692

Dedicated to
William Demarest

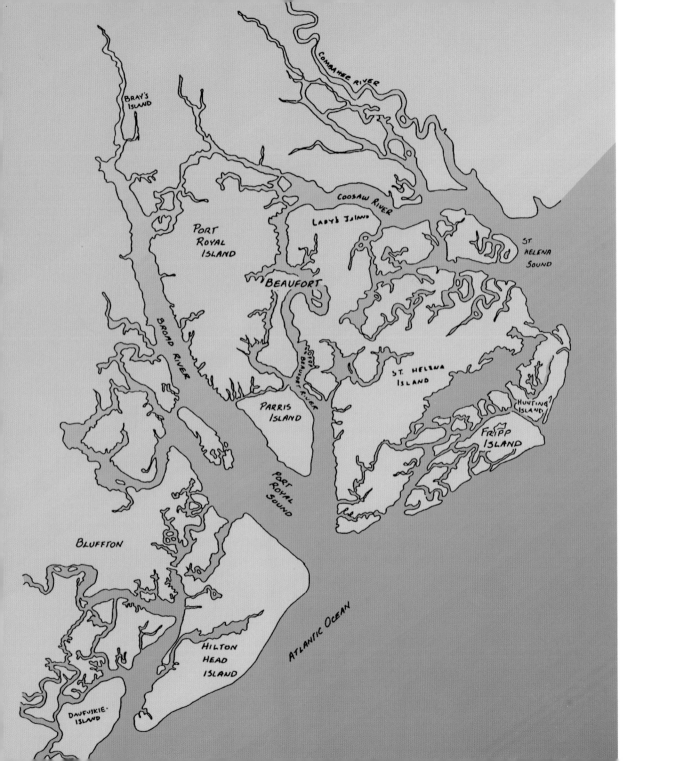

Contents

Acknowledgments

The author wishes gratefully to acknowledge the following individuals and organizations for their assistance and encouragement which did much to help this book become a reality.

Bill and Lynn Michaels, Firehouse Books and Espresso Bar, Beaufort, South Carolina; Lillian Jennings, Director of the Greater Beaufort Arts Advisory Commission; Emory Campbell, Executive Director of Penn Center; Lawrence S. Rowland, Professor of History at the University of South Carolina at Beaufort; Thomas M. Poland, Joan Baldwin, and Mary Whisonant.

I especially want to thank Gerhard Spieler and Ruth Spieler who participated enthusiastically in the conception of this book, providing valuable information and suggestions. Gerhard Spieler also provided essential contributions to the text.

Preface

This book is about Beaufort, South Carolina, the town, and the surrounding islands which encompass the area known as Beaufort County. South of the Combahee River which forms the county's northern border, lies a succession of more than one hundred islands, some well known; others not so well known. They are all separated by rivers and estuaries, creeks, and tiny streams running through a vast salt marshland. This configuration makes the Sea Islands of Beaufort County; the paramount town is Beaufort on Port Royal Island. The Intracoastal Waterway which connects the northern and southern ends of the county is a boulevard for all types of shipping, from heavily-laden barges to cruise ships to pleasure boats both large and small.

It is the rising and falling tide which measures how the islander spends time, makes money, and pursues a particular lifestyle. The shrimping season begins in June and lasts until January; the oysterman begins searching for oyster beds in October and continues until late April. The crabber works year round. These pursuits depend on the tide.

Today this unique area is changing. The sweet-grass basket weaver is hard to find and the art, originally brought over from Africa, is dying out. Changes are taking place constantly, and in some cases, rapidly. Causeways and connecting bridges have been built to reach the more remote islands, and, although the lacework of waterways is still there, life on these islands is quite different from what it used to be.

The Sea Islands constitute an Atlantic Ocean coastal barrier running from Fort George Island, Florida, to the Santee Delta in South Carolina. The jewel of the Sea Islands, in my belief, is that island-studded area within Beaufort County which is nourished by two inlets of the Atlantic, Port Royal Sound and St. Helena Sound. These two large sounds cause the flood and ebb of the tides to dominate the Sea Islands of Beaufort County.

The end papers of this book show a map of Beaufort County indicating how much of the area is open water, estuaries, creeks, and tidal marshlands. My book's purpose is to offer a cultural and environmental presentation of Beaufort County while it is in transition. It is essentially a pictorial presentation, with chapter introductions by Gerhard Spieler, that strives to catch the mood and mystique of Beaufort County. It is addressed not only to residents of Beaufort and adjacent counties but also to visitors — whether they come by bus or auto, cruise ship or yacht — and to the many others who recognize that there is something intriguingly unique about these Sea Islands.

EbbTide–Flood Tide

A storm approaches Lady's Island.

Introduction

But such a tide as moving seems asleep,
Too full for sound and foam,
When that which drew from out the boundless deep
Turns again home.

"Crossing the Bar"
Alfred Tennyson

There is something providential about the tide surging twice daily to every corner of Beaufort County. Just as the tide first separated the Sea Islands from the continent, today it insulates and distinguishes the area from other parts of the state. For centuries, the tide hampered communications and kept Beaufort out of the mainstream of the state's development. The resultant insularity forged the Beaufort area's strong character.

The tide's bounty is legendary. Shrimp, oysters, and crabs sustained hardy frontiersmen. Today, shellfish sustain marine industries. The tide helps shape the Beaufort area's broad marshes and creeks along whose shores history has long marched. For over four hundred years, the history of the Port Royal area, like the tide, has ebbed and flooded, alternately elevating Beaufort County to a position of prominence, then gently or violently lowering it to insignificance.

In the one and one-half centuries before the first permanent English settlement of Carolina, the French, Spanish, and English vied for the Port Royal area. In the years when the only Europeans who frequented the southern coast were mariners, Port Royal's recognizable headland (Hilton Head) and deepest natural harbor on the southern coast (Port Royal Sound) provided them haven.

In 1562, the "largeness and Fairness thereof" inspired French adventurer Jean Ribaut to call the harbor Port Royal, a name that was appropriate to the "greatest ships of France." The land, he wrote, nurtured "mighty oaks and infinite stores of cedar." Turkeys, partridges, bears, and panthers inhabited the surrounding islands. The land indeed proved bountiful, but it was the sea's abundance that was most remarkable. The Frenchman noted that "two drafts of the net were sufficient to feed all the company of our two ships for a whole day."

Ribaut chose Port Royal in 1562 as the site of the first Protestant colony in North America.

Though the French colony was short lived, the area remained important to European adventurers. In 1564, the Spaniard Pedro Menéndez de Aviles established a presidio named San Felipe and a mission called Santa Elena at a site Ribaut's men had abandoned, a site to be known later as Parris Island.

For the next two decades, Santa Elena was the northernmost of the Spanish Indian missions emanating from St. Augustine. During those years, San Felipe's garrisons served as the last guardian outpost for Spanish treasure fleets coasting northward before turning east across the Atlantic for Cádiz.

Spanish galleons attracted English sea dogs, and in 1587 Sir Francis Drake's ravages forced the Spanish to withdraw from the Port Royal area to St. Augustine. That encounter initiated competition for the Port Royal area which went unresolved for nearly two centuries. By 1650, Spanish Franciscans had returned to Santa Elena, claiming the Port Royal area as the northern boundary of Spanish Florida.

English entrepreneurs intent on establishing a colonial foothold in Carolina visited the Spaniards. William Hilton arrived first, in 1663. Three years later Robert Sanford followed and recommended Port Royal as the best site for the first English colony in Carolina. When Sanford departed, he left behind Dr. Henry Woodward, the man who would become the first English settler of South Carolina.

In 1669, Woodward met an English fleet bound from Barbados to Carolina. Woodward's experience with the Spaniards and Indians proved invaluable. He may have been the man, in fact, who persuaded those first English colonists not to contest the Spaniards' claim to Port Royal. The English sailed north and settled at a more distant, more defendable (albeit less desirable) site which they named Charles Town in honor of their king. (The city was renamed Charleston in 1783.) Colonial diplomacy, it turns out, prevented Port Royal from being South Carolina's oldest city.

Military frontier pressures led to the construction of a fort on Port Royal Island in 1706. It proved to be a natural gathering place for the English and Scottish traders, and in 1711 the Lords Proprietors chartered the town of Beaufort, South Carolina's second oldest town. No sooner had the community been established than it was destroyed in the 1715 Yemassee Indian war, a war that disrupted the Sea Island frontier for the next thirteen years.

Charles Town authorities improved the Port Royal area's defenses, but the establishment of Georgia and Savannah's settlement in 1733 proved

to be the most important contributions to Port Royal's security. Beaufort no longer represented the southern frontier of British North America, though the outbreak of war with Spain renewed old insecurities.

The colonial war's end in 1763 ushered in the first period of real prosperity for the Port Royal area. From 1763 to 1776, the area's population quadrupled. The economy kept pace with the population and the area became a notable shipbuilding center. Beaufort also became prominent for its political conservatism.

The Port Royal area's reconstruction following the American Revolution moved slowly. Prior to the Revolution, the most widely produced money crop in the Sea Islands had been indigo. The war erased the British Empire's indigo bounty, and it took the introduction of sea island cotton in the 1790s to spur the economy to recovery. After the turn of the nineteenth century, cotton was responsible for one of the longest periods of wealth and prosperity in Beaufort's history.

The period from 1800 to 1860 was considered by at least one section of the population to be Beaufort's golden age. By the Civil War the white population was made up almost exclusively of wealthy and refined families. Local planters growing rich on cotton slowly replaced the middle-class yeomen of the Sea Island colonial era. Wealth, concentrated in the hands of a few great families, produced men of mark in politics, scholarship, and religion.

Affluence born of cotton led to the construction of many of the fine houses now gracing Beaufort's National Historic District. During this period, Beaufort gained a reputation for having some of the best libraries and finest schools in the South. Although cotton-based wealth produced this prominence, the planters alone could not produce the cotton. They depended on ever-increasing legions of black laborers, whose enslavement was the most intolerable incongruity of American democracy and the greatest tragedy in our national history.

Beaufort's prominent men threw the full force of their wealth and talent behind the South's hopeless defense of slavery and several achieved national reputations for their efforts. Among them were Robert W. Barnwell, William Elliott III, and William J. Grayson. The most famous of Beaufort's eminent men during these years was the eloquent and obstinate secessionist Robert Barnwell Rhett (1800–1876). Rhett was an attorney general of South Carolina, a U.S. Representative, and then a

U.S. Senator. He was briefly considered as a possible candidate for President of the Confederacy because of his long and consistent advocacy of secession. Unfortunately, in the years when Beaufort gained some national prominence, its reputation rested largely on its defense of a doomed social system.

Beaufort's "Periclean Age" came to a swift and thunderous end on November 7, 1861. At the outset of the Civil War, naval strategists in Washington quickly recognized what their English, French, and Spanish counterparts had known centuries before: that the deepest natural harbor on the Southern coast was also the least capable of being defended from the landward side. They dispatched Commodore Samuel F. DuPont with a strong fleet to secure the Sea Islands for the Union. By circling his squadron in the entrance to Port Royal, DuPont was able to keep up a continuous fusillade on Forts Walker (Hilton Head Island) and Beauregard (Bay Point) while his ships were under fire from the forts for only a few minutes at a time. The forts were soon reduced; the Sea Island planters fled inland.

During the Civil War, the Sea Island slaves became the first "freedmen" in the nation. Following the war, they dominated the culture and politics of the community for many years. Their principal leader, Robert Smalls, was a black U.S. congressman representing South Carolina until 1886. He was also the man who persuaded the United States government to purchase Parris Island for use as a naval coaling station.

In the post-Civil War period, a catastrophic natural disaster visited Beaufort. Though the 1893 hurricane's effects on the Sea Islands were never adequately recorded, the loss of life and property proved enormous. Some contemporary estimates reach as many as fourteen thousand lives lost. The tide again played the decisive role. The wind blew from the east, and when the high tide began to turn, the wind prevented it from ebbing. Disaster struck when a second high tide rolled in, driven by winds in excess of one hundred miles per hour. Ten to twelve feet of water inundated the outlying islands, destroying most farms and dwellings. The twentieth century dawned upon a Beaufort that was again recovering from a serious setback.

During this century, Beaufort has been largely isolated from the mainstream of national and state development. Its railroad was a spur of the old Charleston and Western Carolina line and its highway was the dead end of today's U.S. 21, connected to the mainland by one narrow bridge. Some cotton was grown early in the century, but the

industry succumbed to the price collapse following World War I and the 1919 boll weevil devastation. Some phosphate mines were still operating at the turn of the century, but they finally gave way to competition from Florida. The seafood industry began to represent more than mere sustenance, but it, too, suffered economic fluctuations. Port Royal harbor could still handle sea-going ships, but little was being shipped out of Charleston or Savannah, let alone Port Royal. The Great Depression hurt Beaufort as it did almost all rural areas in the nation. But World War II, with its resultant build-up at the Marine Corps Recruit Training Depot, Parris Island, and the construction of the U.S. Marine Corps Air Station (MCAS Beaufort) north of town during the war, helped break Beaufort County out of the Depression.

Since World War II, Beaufort has largely depended on the federal government for its economic well-being. Traditionally divided into two communities, black and white, Beaufort added a third community — that of the military families. The federal payroll sustained the Sea Island economy in the postwar years; servicemen and civil service workers constituted the only substantial body of middle-class citizens in the county. The large number of widely traveled families proved to be a cultural stimulus. As a result, Beaufort possesses a more cosmopolitan character than most towns its size in South Carolina. The many military personnel who retire in Beaufort have provided the community an influx of permanent contributing citizens.

Beaufort is the Low Country's cultural center. That tradition, which began before the Civil War, continues today. A performing arts center, the Orchestra Guild, the Beaufort Little Theatre, and the Art Association bring cultural diversity to the area, as do the Byrne Miller Dance Theatre and the University of South Carolina at Beaufort. Recent Hollywood feature films shot on location in the Beaufort area continue the tradition of cultural stimulation.

During the 1970s and 1980s, Hilton Head Island gained national prominence as a resort community. Following the construction of a bridge to the mainland in 1956, Hilton Head has grown from a handful of permanent residents to a thriving city. Hilton Head has helped give Beaufort County one of the highest growth rates in the state during the past two decades.

One of the Southeast's most scenic islands, Daufuskie, now faces development similar to that of Hilton Head. Daufuskie's future is, however,

unclear, and controversy surrounds the island's development. Balancing the island's history in the face of progress has drawn a line between island residents and those would develop it. The juxtaposition of immensely wealthy people with people who live in rusting trailers and rotting wooden houses is at best awkward and certainly embarrassing. Still, the modern world slowly seeks to integrate Daufuskie into its ranks while the lyrical language of Gullah floats over this quaint island six miles long and three miles wide.

Controversy and change. These constants have long distinguished the Beaufort area's history. The two qualities that truly represent the essence of the Beaufort area, however, are a rich heritage and abundant natural beauty. Thus, Beaufort is a favorite stop for many as they travel down the East Coast, whether by land or water.

This introduction is based on Lawrence S. Rowland's essay, "But Such a Tide" in Franklin Ashley, Ed., *Faces of South Carolina* (Columbia, 1974) with editorial changes by Thomas M. Poland.

Facing page:
An aerial view reveals how
intertwining rivers and creeks weave
treelike patterns across the Low Country.

Rivers, Creeks
& Estuaries

Like a jewel, Beaufort is firmly set within the rich confines of salt marshes and river-fed estuaries, rivers and estuaries that have long shaped the appearance and the culture of the region.

The story of how all this came to be is the story of geography and geology. Large rivers with abundant flow carry ample sediments and usually form deltas from the alluvial materials they drop at their mouths. Such is the case with the Santee River and its famous delta. Smaller rivers carry much less sediment. Estuaries or deep embayments usually develop where such rivers enter the ocean. Thus, St. Helena Sound and Port Royal Sound formed as they did, where they did: near Beaufort. And their depth and accessibility attracted early explorers.

The deep-water sounds and bays of Beaufort were among North America's first to be explored for colonization by the Spanish, French, and English. In 1664, Captain William Hilton, caught up in the beauty of the area, wrote this desciption: "The air is clean and sweet, the country very pleasant and delightful." Colonists followed, and in due time planters erected mansions and pursued lifestyles of elegance within view of the very rivers and estuaries that to this day paint the region in natural shades of green and blue.

As they did in the era of the explorer, and later the era of the planter, the rivers flowing near Beaufort cut intricate patterns within the marshes. Safely protected in the lee of sheltering barrier islands, marsh grasses ripple before the wind, and the sweet, clean aroma of salt marsh fills the Low Country air. Incoming and outgoing tides circulate rich, essential nutrients through the tidal mazes, thus sustaining the highly productive nursery of the sea: the estuary.

Life-giving arteries, the tides run deep through the region, bringing an abundance of life that springs from the sea to the more inland recesses of the region. The sea's bounty has always meant much to the people of Beaufort, still does, always will.

Barges and other commercial craft laden with cargo travel the Intracoastal Waterway flowing past Beaufort.

Facing page:
Cruise ships bound for scenic sites regularly stop at Beaufort.

Beaufort River separates Lady's Island from Port Royal Island, location of the town of Beaufort.

Recreational and commercial sea craft ply Port Royal waters as regularly as the tide.

The swing bridge yields to one of the countless yachts passing by Beaufort.

11

*Abandoned by a retreating tide,
oysters and tidal pools await a
life-renewing surge of sea water.*

*Mists rise from an incoming tide dominating
all in its path.*

*Facing page:
An old Beaufort mansion, "The Castle," stands
its ground against a high tide.*

At Lady's Island a solitary egret stalks the shallows of high tide beneath a crimson sun.

The reflection of Beaufort's "Little Taj" shimmers across Historic District tidal waters.

15

Companion yachts anchored at midtide await nightfall over Lady's Island.

Facing page:
Pilings and sailboats emerge from the mists of a Low Country morning.

Sporting fall colors, bald cypresses — stately trees of the Low Country — cast their reflections across a flooding Combahee River.

16

Above: Ebenezer Coffin built the Coffin Plantation House in 1800. Today
live oaks and palmettos partially conceal the stately house.

Facing page:
Locally made, a hand-crafted bateau awaits use at
St. Helena Island's Club Creek.

Plantations

Owning land played an important role in determining social status in seventeenth-century Europe. From the first settler's arrival, the same held true in South Carolina. A hereditary nobility based on the creation of large estates found support from the English philosopher John Locke who drew up a set of laws for the new province of Carolina called the "Fundamental Constitutions."

John Locke's grand design was soon abandoned, but the idea of large landed estates retained its attraction. Wealthy planters erected impressive mansions and pursued elegant lifestyles. Large plantations assumed a sound economic basis with the introduction of crops such as indigo and rice, for which much land was needed. However, to work the large tracts of land, numerous fieldhands were necessary.

American Indian and European forced labor proved unsuitable in the hot, humid climate of the Low Country. Importing African slaves solved this problem, and by 1750 a plantation system firmly dependent on slaves had been established in tidewater South Carolina. The system survived until the Civil War.

Following the battle of Port Royal on November 7, 1861, the Confederacy lost most of the Carolina Low Country to the Union. Using the Direct Tax

Act, the United States Federal Government confiscated almost all of the land and real property in St. Helena Parish.

The plantation system was dealt yet another blow by General William Tecumseh Sherman's Special Field Order No. 15 on January 16, 1865. This order designated the coastal area extending thirty miles inland from Florida's St. Johns River to Charleston, South Carolina, for settlement by Negroes. All "abandoned property" was to be taken up by displaced freedmen from other areas in tracts of up to forty acres. Land already sold as a result of the

"Trunks" like this one were once common at rice fields. The surging action of the incoming tide would open the trunk and flood the field. At ebb tide, water pinned the trunk shut, keeping water in the fields.

Facing page:
Northern Beaufort County's Twickenham Plantation resulted from three land grants made in 1732 and 1733.

United States direct tax laws was exempted. Thus, many of the prewar plantations were broken up into smaller tracts of land. "Forty acres and a mule," however, was a promise the federal government was unable to keep.

On December 6, 1865, General Rufus Saxton, the abolitionist commandant of the Port Royal area reported that most of the land held by the post-Civil War Freedmen's Bureau had been returned to the former owners. However, at the end of 1868, only 75,000 acres of an original 312,000 acres seized had been returned. Confusing and contradictory land policies produced tragic results. The antebellum plantation owners saw their lands confiscated, and only a few in the Port Royal area succeeded in reclaiming them. Many of Beaufort's old plantations thus vanished with the Civil War, though some continue to provide a means of cartographic reference. Many of the old plantation names linger on, printed on current maps of Beaufort County: Frogmore, Coffin Point, Bonny Hall, Castle Hill, Tomotly, Bray's Island, Huspah, Coosaw, Brickyard Point, and Hog Bluff Plantation.

Facing page:
Wild mustard adorns the
grounds of an old plantation house.

Peering outward from St. Helena Island's Seaside Plantation, the visitor is greeted by a haunting view of Club Creek.

Facing page:
Sheldon Church ruins. Destroyed by the British in 1779, rebuilt in 1826, and razed again in 1865, Sheldon Church represents an attempt to imitate a Greek temple.

An avenue of live oaks — a classic scene from the South — leads to St. Helena Island's Coffin Point Plantation.

Live oaks and Spanish moss make for a quaint lane — and the route to Seaside Plantation at St. Helena Island.

At Twickenham Plantation the buttressed cypress trunks provide a firm base for trees anchored in a soft bottom alternately in and out of water.

The Islands

*Above: Viewed from Land's End at St. Helena Island, a setting sun colors
the sky above Hilton Head.*

Facing page:
*Tombee Plantation looks out over St. Helena Island's Station Creek. The old
house sits high and dry on a tabby foundation, built circa 1790.*

Over sixty-eight "large" islands lie off the coast of Beaufort, and more than two hundred smaller isles, at least a half acre in size, dot the salty stretches. Hundreds of even smaller knolls speckle the tidal marshes. As the tide washes in and out, the edges of islands and marshes submerge, then resurface. In all, three hundred additional acres grace Beaufort County at ebb tide; high tide washes these same three hundred acres from sight with regular predictability.

The islands form part of the great Sea Island complex that extends from the Santee Delta over one hundred miles to the Savannah River. Diverse in size, development, and origin, these lovely islands distinguish the waters off Beaufort. Two types of islands comprise Beaufort's Sea Islands. St. Helena, being inland from the ocean, is classified as an erosional remnant. It was once solidly connected to the mainland. Hunting Island and Fripp Island bear the name barrier island. Sand dune systems and beach ridges anchor these islands whose origin may be due to either the formation of offshore sandbars or a fluctuating coastline during the Pleistocene Epoch.

Ever-shifting dunes give the islands a transient character. As the wind goes, so go the dunes. Majestic sea oats (synonymous with sand dunes) move with the wind while helping to stabilize the transient mounds. On both types of islands, sea oats perform this very valuable function. So valuable that the law protects them from those who would rather see them in dried arrangements.

The largest island, Port Royal, so christened by Jean Ribaut, supports the town of Beaufort on its easternmost tip. Other large islands include Hilton Head, Daufuskie, St. Helena, Lady's Island, Hunting, and Fripp. The major islands within this chain possess singular histories. While the mainland forged its own unique history, the Sea Islands took no back seat.

Morning mists slowly burn off, revealing the town of Beaufort.

Overlooking the Beaufort River is the Lewis Reeves house, built in 1852. This house serves as a good example of Beaufort-style architecture adapted to the Greek Revival period.

Bay Street view of the Beaufort River, marshes, and marina.

Above and facing page:
"The Castle," so named because of its formidable
appearance and ample use of brick and stucco.

Roger Pinckney, Beaufort County coroner for thirty-five years and an adept woodcarver, sports the shillelagh he fashioned from crepe myrtle.

36

Tidalholm, nearly surrounded by water, commands a mighty view of the Beaufort River.

In a manner befitting the period, newlyweds
tour The Point in the historic district.

Ancient oaks and their spreading branches gave the name to the house aptly called "The Oaks" in the historic district.

39

Mr. Wilson "Tootie" Burke, once named Beaufort Citizen of the Year as well as honorary patrolman by the Beaufort Police Department

Byrne Miller brought modern dance to Beaufort audiences, to the schools, and to the handicapped.

Lady's Island

Lady's Island lies across from the town of Beaufort, readily accessible via either of the bridges from Port Royal Island. The origin of the island's name is clouded. Early Spanish explorers referred to the place as the Island of Our Lady, and this is one possible explanation for the name.

Almost three hundred years ago, this island's large fields supported cattle and indigo. Lord and Lady Askell of England owned the island and its cattle and indigo plantations in 1710, so perhaps Lady's Island was named for Lady Askell.

Whatever the source of the name, a dispute thrived for many years as to the correct spelling of it: Lady's or Ladies Island? The controversy reached all the way to Washington, D.C., and the spelling settled upon is the one in use today.

Facing page:
Yachts peacefully moored in their slips at
Marsh Harbor stand ready to let the wind take
them out over historic waters.

Jackie Ford of Beaufort Marina feels at home on the waterfront. With pipe and Greek fisherman's cap, he looks the part of an "old salt."

St. Helena Island

St. Helena Island lies just southeast of Lady's Island. On August 18, 1525, St. Helen's Day, Pedro de Quexos landed on an island the Spaniards called Punta de Santa Elena. When English planters subdued the Spaniards, they changed the name to St. Helena.

Much of the land on St. Helena Island is owned by black families dating back many years. Blacks, consistently in the majority from about 1730 to the present, speak the Gullah dialect, as beautiful to hear as it is unique.

Penn Community Services, Inc., formerly Penn School, was established on the island in 1862 during the Civil War to educate the freedmen of St. Helena and the surrounding areas of the Low Country. This school has served as a model for similar institutions in South Africa.

Old tabby remains hint at St. Helena's past, remains such as those of the White Church. A small community named Frogmore distinguishes St. Helena Island. Traveling through the island, a winding road runs through marshes and by picturesque live oaks, a setting prompting one to think of the island's past.

The old general store lives on: Mabe's Store, located in Frogmore, sells Frogmore souvenir T-shirts, ice, groceries, and more.

Above left:
Emory S. Campbell, Executive Director of Penn Center, leads an ongoing effort by Beaufort citizens — black and white — to give all an education.

Above right:
Deacon David Henderson cares for the last Praise House, a sanctuary where slaves could gather and worship.

Left:
Lilly Singleton carries on the making of sweet-grass baskets, an art brought from Africa by the slaves and now inextricably tied to the Low Country.

Emory Campbell stands by the old Brick Church, built in 1855 for Baptist planters. The church served as an early location of the Penn School and housed as well the very first school for blacks in the South.

Hilton Head Island

Of all the islands in the Sea Island complex, a boot-shaped, forty-two-square-mile area called Hilton Head is the most famous, enjoying an international reputation. In 1950, the population of Hilton Head amounted to but a few hundred souls. By 1980, well over eleven thousand people considered Hilton Head Island home, and, no doubt, by the next census, the number will have grown even more, a surge due to tourism and retirees settling in the area.

English planters domiciled in Barbados and Bermuda sent Captain William Hilton to explore the Carolina coast. William Hilton set sail August 10, 1663, on the ship *Adventure* . Upon observing a noteworthy landmark that was to become Hilton Head, he noted "the headland is bluft." Thus, the name Hilton Head.

Over the years other Englishmen followed Hilton, and in time a prosperous group of plantations sprang up. As time passed and the American Revolution loomed on the horizon, politics assumed paramount importance. The politics of Hilton Head were those of the Whig Patriots. The neighboring island, Daufuskie, espoused the politics of the Tories. When the American Revolution heated up, these neighboring islands kept a wary eye on each other.

Hilton Head flourished until the Civil War. The island then experienced a lengthy decline until the famous Sea Pines Resort was developed there in the mid-1950s. Other developments followed, and today Hilton Head is synonymous with luxury and a genteel way of living.

Facing page:
Braddock's Point, named for a colonial planter, bristles with condominiums and marinas today.

This page:
Lynn Livingston Smith, known as "Buck" or "Daddy," was born on Hilton Head where he ran an oyster cannery and served as a magistrate.

Following page:
Harbour Town, a man-made harbor, ranks as one of Hilton Head's notable landmarks.

Daufuskie Island

Daufuskie, the most isolated of all the islands, is accessible only by boat. A picturesque island, its name derives from the language of the Muskhogean Indians. As late as 1972, little was known about Daufuskie Island. Since that time, developers have acquired this semitropical barrier island situated between Beaufort and Savannah. The 1970 population of the island, according to the census, was 112. Planned residential communities referred to as "plantations" seem to be the future of Daufuskie. An influx of people is estimated to drive the island's population to somewhere around ten thousand by the year 2000. Times are changing on Daufuskie. Vanishing are the days when the island's meager population of black people would increase on weekends when Savannah residents ferried over to get away from civilization for a while.

Today Daufuskie Island is no longer as far off the beaten track. Tour boats offer excursions to this island where two major developments are in progress. Lingering evidence of the prosperous antebellum times remains, remnants of old homes, churches, and schools. Daufuskie's great wealth of wildlife and pristine habitat remind us how such islands must have appeared before settlement. Even though development is transforming the island, cattle remain the principal users of the island's narrow, dusty, single-lane roads. This, too, will soon be different. The winds of change are blowing across Daufuskie.

*Silver Dew Winery, abandoned. Fragrant
smells drifted through these doors in the
early part of the twentieth century as island-
grown grapes were made into wine.*

*Facing page:
A steep tin roof and a chimney at
one end mark the architecture of
houses quaintly referred to as
"tenant homes."*

Remnants of a maritime forest lie on the beach at Bloody Point. On the southeastern tip of Daufuskie, this spot was the site of an Indian massacre.

Hunting Island

Hunting Island confronts the sea as a barrier island. The Atlantic works at washing away the north end of the island. At the south end, a hiking trail winds its way along a sand ridge. This secluded domain of tree-fringed beaches and semi-tropical woodlands once known as Reynolds Island hosts a five-thousand-acre state park located approximately sixteen miles from Beaufort. It offers more than three miles of Atlantic beaches where abundant hiking and nature trails provide splendid opportunities for exploration. Hunting Island State Park may well be the most popular state park in South Carolina. Well over one million people a year visit this seaside park which boasts one of the finest natural public beaches on the eastern shore.

The centerpiece of the island is a fascinating lighthouse built in 1875 but abandoned in 1933. Climbing its 181 steps to the top (136 feet above ground) rewards the energetic visitor with a sweeping view of the ocean, the island, and adjacent marshes. A rolling surf washes onto a white border of sand. A variety of shorebirds inhabit the beach. Laughing gulls fight the wind while ruddy turnstones turn their backs to the breeze. A maritime forest then greets the eye. The state tree, the cabbage palmetto, abounds. Turning to the back side of the island, one finds a thick growth of salt marsh.

A historic lighthouse stands guard over Hunting Island, one of the most popular state parks in the Low Country, if not in the state.

The original Hunting Island lighthouse was built in 1859 but destroyed by beach erosion. The current lighthouse went up in 1875 a mile and a quarter south of the original site.

Surf washes inland where a proud maritime forest
once stood, testament to the sea's persistence.

Facing page:
Undisturbed marshland, some of the
planet's most productive habitat.

Soon the effects of surf and wind
will topple this pine; then the
sea's pounding will break it
apart and push it ashore.

Facing page:
Beach erosion has reduced the
remnants of a maritime forest to
mere snags in the sand.

Fripp Island

Once known as Prentis, then named for John Fripp, a St. Helena Island planter and surveyor, Fripp Island supports a three-thousand-acre resort and residential community. The smooth white beaches of Fripp might have borne the footprints of a legendary figure: Edward Teach, a pirate better known as Blackbeard. As legend has it, Blackbeard chose Fripp Island as his hideaway because its maze of creeks and inlets provided sanctuary from those seeking to locate him. Yet another legend has it that Count Casimir Pulaski, a cavalry commander in the American Revolution, is buried here. After receiving a mortal wound at Savannah, he died on board a ship en route from there and purportedly was interred on Fripp Island.

Facing page:
A rising sun breaks over the Atlantic,
the start of another island day.

64

Sea oats, sentinels of the beach, watch over the paths taken by beach strollers.

Parris Island

South of Beaufort lies Parris Island, which has the longest history of all the islands and is well known as the location of the Parris Island Marine Recruit Depot. In 1891, a small detachment of marines serving at a naval station began what would grow to be a full-fledged training battalion. Each year approximately twenty-five thousand young men who hail from east of the Mississippi River and all young women bound for a marine enlisted career get their first taste of rigorous military training on Parris Island.

It is not known for certain who first settled the island. It was long believed that the French Huguenots, led by Jean Ribaut, were the first to land, arriving in 1562 to establish Charles Fort. Supposedly Ribaut left a garrison of soldiers to build the fort. In 1979, however, University of South Carolina archaeologists unearthed artifacts indicating that the Spanish arrived first. It is now generally held that Spanish seafarers discovered the island in the 1500s. In 1670, the English arrived. In 1715, Alexander Parris, public treasurer of South Carolina, acquired the island and renamed it Parris Island. Parris Island was also the site of many working plantations, the first of which was established in 1735 by the son-in-law and daughter of Alexander Parris.

Visitors to Parris Island tour the military training center where they can also see the War Memorial Building Museum which features a collection of vintage uniforms, photographs, weapons, and special exhibits. Of particular interest is the replica of the monument depicting the raising of the U.S. flag on Iwo Jima during World War II.

*Women marines snake beneath barbed wire barricades, a routine
that is part of their combat training.*

A proud moment, an emotional moment, a Marine Corps graduation.

69

Bray's Island

Unlike the sea islands, Bray's Island sits inland. Like the sea islands, it possesses a unique history. Indians, Spanish, French, and English march through the history of this island. In 1521, Vásquez Ayllón explored the area. Eighteen years later, DeSoto traveled through the region. From descriptions provided in historical accounts written by William Hilton, it is most likely that he, too, explored the island in 1663. It is another William, however — William Bray — whose name identifies Bray's Island today. An Indian trader, he lived in the vicinity of the island with his family.

During the Revolutionary War, the Bray's Island area was the site of battles between British and American forces. Though the war caused hardship in the area, rice and cotton led the way for prosperity, which dramatically increased with the advent of the cotton gin in 1790.

As the Civil War wound down, the parish in which Bray's Island is located, Prince William's Parish, found itself right in the path of Sherman's army, and the area was leveled. From the time of the Civil War through the remainder of the century, Bray's Island and the adjacent area suffered.

When the Low Country and the Sea Islands grew in stature as vacation spots and areas for high-density development, Bray's Island was purchased for development as a modern-day plantation. Today this island is a private community. Where Indians once grew squash and corn, grain crops now nurture horses and coveys of quail.

Facing page:
Azaleas festoon the yard of The Inn,
formerly the home of Mr. and Mrs.
Sumner Pingree.

Quail hunting, a Low Country tradition, challenges novice and veteran.

Rufus Pinckney, born on Bray's Island, poles his craft down river.

The Pocotaligo River slips past the marshland and the remnants of a gnarled live oak forlornly stranded at marsh's edge.

Spanish moss framing a Fripp Island tidal pond gives it a decidedly Low Country air.

Life in the Low Country

Consider the tools necessary to harvest the sea's delicacies awaiting in Beaufort's saltwater creeks and estuaries. A chicken neck and a dip net. A hoe and a wooden basket. A cast net. Steel bars and sacks. A rod and reel. These tools are all you need to gather blue crabs, clams, shrimp, oysters, and game fish such as spot, channel bass, and flounder.

The sea's culinary treasures have long enriched the Port Royal Sound area. Captain William Hilton praised the vast amounts of clams, crabs, and oysters, but ironically, he dismissed the surrounding marshes as worthless, a lesson people have only begun to unlearn.

Witness Beaufort's colorful Low Country fishing scenarios . . .

Blue crabs. . . Nothing is more colorful than a clattering basket of Atlantic blue crabs. They hang perilously by single claws to the sides of a crude chicken-wire basket before being transferred to a bubbling pot of hot water which turns them orange.

Clams . . . The clammer rises early. Armed with hoe and bucket, he searches for clams, a basket at his side.

Whiting and spot . . . Surf fishermen wade out to their hips. Their graceful casts send shimmering lines splashing into the surf. Nearby, a creek cuts

through the marsh. Along its distant edge, oyster banks catch the rising sun's first rays. Not far away, a porpoise chases creek shrimp.

A shimmering cast net catches the sun before plopping into the water. A few tugs on the net and a handsome catch of shrimp, a solitary crab, and some small fish come wiggling ashore.

A receding tide exposes oysters. Well-placed blows from a steel rod break loose clusters. Bushel baskets begin to fill. Later, whether cooked in a smoker or roasted over a fire, the oysters go down easily.

Crabbing

Anyone walking Beaufort County's summer beaches soon realizes that jumbo Atlantic blue crabs abound in creeks, estuaries, and the ocean itself. During a normal life span of two or three years, female blue crabs usually spawn twice, producing up to four million eggs.

Favorable conditions promote rapid growth and crabs hatched in May increase in size about three inches by November. Twelve months after hatching, crabs reach the commercial size of a carapace of five inches or more.

A familiar sight is that of a crabber with net in

hand and a chicken neck tied to a string. Fling the chicken neck into the water, and be patient. A blue crab is sure to come along. A quick scoop of the net snares the crab and he joins other unfortunate colleagues in a basket. Once the crabbing is done, it's time to steam the crabs for a true Low Country treat.

Fishing

Beaufort's deep-water bays and sounds provided some of America's earliest saltwater fishing. To this day, many ways of fishing in the Carolina Low Country exist, ranging from expensive fishing trawlers to homemade elegant flat-bottom bateaux and from sophisticated rods and reels to simple bamboo poles.

In the many saltwater fingers stretching inland in Beaufort County, trout, flounder, whiting, shrimp, and blue crabs abound. Throwing a white cast net out over the fertile waters produces a harvest equal only to the skill of the caster, for casting the round, weighted net is truly a Low Country art.

Channel bass frequent the surf line where surf casters hurl their lures and bait into the tide. Offshore of Beaufort County, the Atlantic Ocean har-

bors mackerel, bonita, and bluefish. Approximately seventy miles offshore, the Gulf Stream nurtures marlin and sailfish, and deep sea fishermen regularly depart the sounds in their quest for these spectacular game fish.

Shrimping

Captain Charles Vecchio was known to the people of Port Royal as "the daddy of the shrimp industry." From 1924 to the early 1930s, he spent alternate years in Beaufort and Florida. He has been quoted as saying "shrimp are very much like birds in their habits. In summer, they are up around Beaufort; for the winter, they go further south and the Florida season is on."

Before his arrival, shrimp had been caught locally mostly in rivers and creeks. Captain Vecchio ventured farther offshore. During the 1931 season, his twenty-two boats caught five hundred thousand pounds of shrimp. Packed in barrels with ice, 125 pounds of shrimp to the barrel, they were shipped fresh to northern markets.

Shrimp boats still ply Beaufort's waters and sounds. State law also permits "casting" of shrimp nets by private individuals for family consumption.

In recent years, commercial shrimpers have been handicapped by the annual fluctuation of catches due to cold snaps, the high price of fuel, and, perhaps, too many shrimp boats competing for the same catch.

Oystering

When the Indians considered the Sea Islands their own, oysters abounded in Beaufort waters. Among the legacies of Indians are mounds of empty oyster shells, some placed in large rings two hundred and fifty feet in diameter and five feet high. The rings perhaps have religious origins, and some of the largest rings possess bases averaging thirty-five feet.

White settlers found the New World oysters larger and tastier than those they ate in Europe. Oysters formed a staple food of the black plantation workers. To this day, oysters remain a delicacy that can be had for the picking by Low Country residents.

Not so very long ago, oyster shells formed the base for many local roads in the area. The road from Beaufort to the town of Port Royal was known as the Shell Road, as was the road running along the western shore of Lady's Island. Oysters also provided a primary source for tabby, the Low Country building material equivalent to today's concrete.

An oyster roast remains among the most enjoyable of regional treats. Held in late fall and winter, this event, with its fare of steamed oysters collected by boatmen in traditional flat-bottom bateaux, proves an unexcelled culinary delight. The specter of water pollution looms on the horizon, however, posing a threat to the simple but elegant oyster. From time to time, various pollutants taint oysters, but the good news is that once the shellfish are relocated to clean water they rapidly rid themselves of pollutants.

The Marshes

A major portion of Beaufort County's 588 square miles consists of water and marshlands. Only recently have the salt marshes been recognized as a vital natural resource. The truth is that emerald marshes and salty mud flats serve as the ocean's nursery. Once, however, they were routinely thought of as mosquito-laden wastelands where deadly miasmas originated.

Not only is a winding, grass-lined creek beautiful to behold; it is also a wondrous thing capable of sustaining a rich variety of sea life. An acre of Nebraska corn or wheat, nurtured and pampered by the latest agricultural techniques and technology, cannot compare with an acre of salt marsh. An acre of salt marsh produces twice as much plant matter in a year as does that acre of Nebraska. The salt marshes stretching green, rippling beneath the wind, may well have the most productive ecosystem on the planet.

Ebb tide, flood tide . . . they flush the decaying plant and organic matter from the marshes into the sea. This detritus, as it's known, provides a vital link in the sea's food chain. Some of the creatures in the marsh live on plankton. Others live on small fish. The food chain goes on until it reaches the top where men live on species such as shrimp, oysters, and fin fish. But salt marshes provide more than just food; they also provide shelter for marine life. Oysters, crabs, and shrimp all depend on the marsh at some point in their lives for shelter. Clam and scallop larvae, for instance, secrete threads which they tie to marsh plants. Shellfish and offshore fish often begin their existence in the marsh. Decaying marsh provides fertilizer for plankton, which in one way or another feeds approximately ninety percent of all saltwater fish and shellfish. It's no coincidence that the salt marshes of Port Royal Sound run rich with cobia. The clean waters support abundant numbers of crustaceans and fish which are the cobia's dining delight.

The marshes stretching out from the Port Royal Sound happen to be one of the richest, unpolluted estuarian systems along the East Coast. Marsh mud and grasses together with bacteria and other forms of life, filter water, clear up most water pollution, absorb inorganic and organic pollutants, and eliminate, as well, the turbidity of coastal waters. Marshes act as buffers against flood tides, storm waves, and storm winds.

For people, the marshes provide not only food but also beautiful scenery highlighted by subtle but never-ending change. Our fragile marshes offer solitude and solace to those of us weary of modern ways. Our hope is that the by-products of modern ways don't destroy the marshes.

Bright green fields and red tomatoes color the month of June when workers harvest the tasty vegetable from Beaufort fields.

Above right:
A proud Rosa Green harvests daffodil buds. Grown in great
quantities and shipped north, the flowers represent yet another
"natural harvest" of the Low Country.

Right:
Mary Owens, manager of the pickers,
shows off a bushel basket of their efforts.

Above left:
Full blossoms open to the sun
prove too tempting for
Miranda, wanderer among the daffodils.

Crabbers pull up a clattering pot of blue crabs intent on escaping their chicken-wire enclosure.

*David Diehl scans the early morning
waters for signs of his pots.*

*Throwing a cast net is a
Low Country art difficult to master but
rewarding for those who do.*

A solitary fisherman tries his luck from his bateau on Chowan Creek.

*"Mud balls" of cornmeal
are used to lure shrimp to net.*

Rufus Pinckney mends nets in Sheldon.

85

Shrimp boats of Frogmore, together for now, will go their separate ways once trawling for shrimp.

A large haul of shrimp comes aboard.

A careened shrimper showing an outrigger against a backdrop of green marsh and blue water.

A shrimper with its outrigger of nets and doors and other shrimpers in the background.

Surrounded by gulls eager for food, "Miss Tiffany" heads home from a successful trawl.

Oysters galore . . . some of the sea's most delectable offerings whether steamed, fried, or raw.

Heavily laden with oysters, a bateau and her oystermen wearily head home, low in the water from the weight of the harvest.

Tonging for oysters, now almost obsolete, has long been a way of life for many Low Country residents.

90

At a dock along the Chechessee River,
oystermen wash down their harvest.

Standing in "pluff mud," and stained by it as well, a rugged oysterman
displays his pleasure at the oyster bank behind him.

91

Henry Robinson,
chef of the oyster roast.

Facing page:
"Tabby Manse," built in 1786, so
named because it is constructed from
tabby, the durable building material
utilizing oyster shells.

Break time for oystermen
who have spent the morning
washing down mounds of oysters.

92

A working shrimp boat.

Facing page:
Sun-dappled and surrounded by dogwood blossoms, the
Barnwell-Gough House was built circa 1786. Nearly
identical to "Tabby Manse" on Bay Street, the entire house
is made of brick and covered with stucco.

*Retreat Plantation, circa 1740, owned by
Jean de la Gaye, a French Huguenot. This tabby
construction is believed to be the oldest plantation residence extant in the Low Country.*

*Ruins of a plantation once
owned by John Cochran.
About 1800, the George Edwards
family inherited the plantation.
Sea island cotton once grew here.*

A live-oak alley leads to the two-storied tabby ruins of the George Edwards plantation house.

97

98   *The Chapel of Ease was built from 1742 to 1747 to care for planters*
who could not come to the mainland. Note the rough texture of the tabby exterior.

These old tabby ruins at Dataw are from the William Sams Plantation, circa 1786.
It looks almost as if an oyster bank grows from the end wall.

The tide is out at Calibogue Marsh on Hilton Head Island.
Soon the tide will move in beneath the limbs of this toppled live oak.

The ruins of Callawassie, thought to
be remnants of an old sugar mill.

*A quiet afternoon along the inland
waterways near Beaufort.*

Epilogue

To know Beaufort is to know her history, her islands, her seaside atmosphere, and her rich culture and to appreciate her salt marshes, islands, sand dunes and sea oats, shrimp trawlers, tabby, and the flowing Gullah dialect.

Beaufort and the surrounding area have long attracted settlers. Their early efforts to establish homes here, to live here resulted in conflict and progress. And while Beaufort's mood may have changed as the storms of nature and human nature have come and gone through the years, her essential character has remained unscathed.

She is a jewel by the seaside, smooth and polished to a beautiful sheen by the passing of the years.

About the Author

Lynn McLaren, photojournalist, received her education from Vassar College and the Missouri School of Photojournalism. Her work has appeared in *Design*, *Yankee*, and *Natural History* magazines, among others.

She has worked on assignment for *Newsweek*, *National Geographic*, *Time*, *Life*, and the *Rockefeller Foundation Quarterly*. Her books include *Berlin and the Berliners; The Village: The People*, a photo essay on village life in India; *Life of a Student Nurse;* and *A Book for Boston*.

Her one-woman shows have been featured around the United States, at the United Nations, and in Washington, D.C., where *Faces of Washington: A Study of a City* appeared.

Ms. McLaren resides in Beaufort, South Carolina.

Facing page:
Looking out? How many have sat in this worn rocker and watched the tide ebb and flood over the marshes of Beaufort?